The Wise Mama Guide to Maternity Leave

Avoid Burnout, "Bad Mom Syndrome," and Other Common Pitfalls of Motherhood

Lisa Abramson

Advanced Praise

"**Down-to-earth and packed with honesty,** this unique guide cuts through layers of damaging motherhood myths. Following the wise tips Lisa Abramson gathered the hard way, new moms and moms-to-be can avoid many common struggles and truly enjoy maternity leave."

- Shoshana Bennett, Ph.D., Perinatal Psychologist and Author of *Postpartum Depression for Dummies*

"**Filled with wisdom, soul, and raw honesty,** this book is the ultimate companion guide for the messy truth behind the mystery of early motherhood."

- Dr. Leslie Carr, Licensed Clinical Psychologist and Mental Health Advocate

"**This is the book I wish I had read before I became a mom.** As a high achieving and independent woman, transitioning to motherhood was challenging. This book is the perfect guide to entering this new phase of life with intention and armed with tips, tools and resources for a smooth transition."

- Suzannah Scully, TEDx Speaker, Executive Coach and Podcast Host

"**Perfect for the busy mom-to-be, there is so much helpful information packed into this concise and easy to digest book.** A MUST read if you are returning to work after the birth of a child."

- Casey Georgeson, Innovation and Creative Lead at The Wine Group

"**This is the manual new moms need for navigating motherhood** and integrating a new baby into our already busy everyday routine. From mindfulness to self-compassion to getting comfortable asking for help, this concise guide teaches life skills all new moms can benefit from learning more about. I highly recommend it."

- Jennifer Marshall, TEDx Speaker and Co-Founder & Executive Director of This is My Brave

Table of Contents

To my daughter Lucy, before you were even conceived, the thought of bringing a little one into this world inspired me to be an entrepreneur and pursue my dreams fearlessly. And since you were born, you've inspired me on a whole new level to be my best self. May you always know how dearly you are loved. And to my husband David, you are my rock and I wouldn't be here without you. I can't imagine a better partner to walk through this journey of love, life and parenthood; you have my heart and always will. And to my parents (all of them), thank you for always believing in me.

CHAPTER 1

When Sh*t Hits The Fan (As It Did For Me)

Sometimes, even with the best preparation and lots of support, things don't go as planned. I had a very challenging time in my first few months as a mom while out on maternity leave. My experience was unique, extreme and thankfully quite rare; but it provided me with a few lessons that I believe can benefit all new moms.

Case in point: a few years ago, I went temporarily insane and was locked in a psychiatric ward for 10 days.

Me, a lifelong overachiever, known for having my sh*t together, spent 10 days confined against my will. I was locked up, marked as "crazy," and I thought, tainted for life.

It wasn't because I had taken a pill in Ibiza. Or because I had a previously undetected mental illness. The reason was quite unexpected; it was because I had become a mom.

One month into motherhood, my world came crashing down around me. I didn't recognize myself in the mirror.

I wasn't the confident and positive woman I used to be. I was exhausted, in a deep fog, and crying all the time. I had started avoiding my friends. Deep down, I knew something was wrong, but I REALLY didn't want to believe something was wrong with me.

As my sleep deprivation got worse, I began to get more and more disoriented. I became erratic, paranoid, and then suicidal.

I thought it was all my fault and that I had done something wrong. I thought for sure my family would abandon me, my daughter would never love me, and my husband would leave me. Why would they want someone who was such a hot mess?

Before being confined, I felt like a failure because I was having trouble breastfeeding. After my confinement, I believed I was not only "crazy," but also the world's worst mom.

I believed I was completely unfit to be a mom, and also unfit to run my business teaching people, ironically, about mindfulness and mental wellbeing. I thought my days working with high potential women leaders, as well as leading workshops at companies like Microsoft, Salesforce, and Google were over.

In hindsight, I had no idea that sleep deprivation, stress and hormonal changes after birth could have such a drastic impact on my brain chemistry.

The months following my hospitalization were intensely challenging, and many times I was brought to my knees as I faced my worst fears, relearned how to question my thoughts, and how to be kinder to myself.

Through a combination of medical, therapeutic and family support, I recovered fully and no longer take any medications. I've also continued to have a thriving career, and have a healthy, wonderful relationship with my daughter, husband and family. I'm so grateful to have found the right support and a well of resilience within me, and now feel stronger and healthier than ever before.

Although my experience was rare, (only 1 in 1,000 new moms experience Postpartum Psychosis), I believe what I learned throughout my recovery can help all new moms, whether they are struggling with postpartum mood concerns or not.

While it would be easier to sweep my experience under the rug, and keep it hidden there forever, I feel called to share it. Every time I share my story I see it spark a dialogue and give women the courage to share their own struggles and to seek help, if they need it. And that's what gives me the courage to share my story with you here, and why I think it's so important to be real and honest about our difficulties.

CHAPTER 2

What Overachieving Types Need To Know About Motherhood

My journey into motherhood officially began on May 2nd, 2013, as I peed on a stick. Said stick confirmed I was pregnant, and I immediately fell in love with the tiny being in my belly.

For as long as I can remember though, I have always been intensely driven; out on the soccer field, in the classroom, and anywhere else I got positive feedback. Whenever I failed, I believed it was because I didn't try hard enough, and then vowed to commit myself more fully the next time around. That way I never really "failed" or experienced disappointment. For example, when I didn't win the election for class president in middle school, I blamed the fact that I had only created two campaign posters instead of ten, and that my slogan "Lisa 4 President" was thrown together very last minute.

But at my best, I've always known how to set a goal and then let nothing get in the way of achieving it. For example, in my first job after college, I decided that getting promoted to Account Executive in the regular one year timeframe was too slow. To get promoted faster, I took on additional projects and clients, I invested my own time and money into improving my writing skills through a night class, and I was always one of the first people in the office. My efforts were noticed, and I was promoted within nine months, instead of the usual year. This pattern of working hard and being rewarded continued for years as I climbed the corporate ladder. It wasn't long before I joined the executive team at a fast growing startup, as the youngest and first female member.

These traits helped me succeed within the corporate world, and I ended up being named one of the 25 "Women to Watch" by a leading trade publication. However, in the longer run, they were also my downfall in facing exhaustion, burnout, and a whole lot of stress.

With corporate stress levels at an all time high, I, and many others, have experienced the devastating effects of burning out. When you're burned out, you might feel high levels of stress and anxiety, have low energy, be exhausted, and feel like there's "never enough time." You may also have frequent negative feelings, feel overwhelmed, be irritable, and lack motivation. In severe situations, you may even stop taking care of yourself, have trouble focusing, and experience a range of health issues. Sadly, it's quite common to not notice that you're suffering from burnout, since it's likely the water you've always swam in.

If you're prone to burnout, or resonate with being an overachiever, or Type A personality, there are some things you need to know about becoming a mom.

In the 1980s, Dr. Herbert Freudenberger, author of *Burnout: The High Cost of High Achievement*[1], was the first person to describe the syndrome known as burnout. Throughout his years of work with high-achieving clients, he uncovered the type of person most likely to burnout.

1. YOU'RE A GOAL FOCUSED OVERACHIEVER.

Once you set a goal, you're relentless about achieving it. Nothing can get in your way. You're capable of moving mountains when you're focused, and have your goal in sight.

2. YOU CAN ALWAYS BE COUNTED ON TO DO MORE THAN YOUR FAIR SHARE, NO MATTER HOW BUSY YOU ARE.

You're a team player, always thinking about what you can give and how you can help out. No matter how overworked and busy you are, you always do your part, and sometimes overextend yourself to fill in for others.

3. YOU'RE A LEADER WHO HAS A HARD TIME ADMITTING LIMITATIONS.

You're effective at leading your team, getting people to see that there is a way, and that there is always hope. You rarely think of any challenges as unconquerable, and believe that with enough effort you can do whatever you put your mind to.

4. YOU PUSH YOURSELF HARD AND GET RESULTS.

You know how to avoid distraction and remain focused. You realize that hard work and dedication are required to accomplish anything meaningful.

Overachievers prone to burnout need to be careful as they transition into the messy waters of motherhood. To succeed in motherhood, overachievers need to let go of some of their old ways and plan for their new, and different reality.

Motherhood is the antithesis of achievement and "success." There are no gold stars for getting things "right." There are also no fixed goals. Oh, and before I forget, motherhood is an ultra marathon as well. As a goal oriented mom-to-be, you might find this mind boggling and confusing. I'm with you, but stay with me.

When I was pregnant, like any good overachiever, I did all I could to prepare myself for the birth of our bundle of joy. I read dozens of books, researched and purchased countless baby products, listened to hypnobirthing audios, attended 35 hours of a Mindfulness Based Childbirth and Parenting class along with my husband, got trained in infant CPR, and sacrificed an entire weekend at a leading newborn care and childbirth preparation training.

But it turned out this prep work wasn't what I so desperately needed. I needed to know more about the life altering identity shift coming my way, how to really let go of work and enjoy my leave, and how my relationship with my husband would drastically change overnight. While I knew I'd be forming a new relationship with my daughter, I didn't know how drastically my relationship with myself would change as I went from a self-sufficient high achieving woman to a mother.

It's time to start a dialogue around motherhood that takes into account that when you become a mom, you don't stop being YOU.

I hope this guide helps make your transition a lot smoother than mine was.

These are my hard earned lessons.

CHAPTER 3

What is Bad Mom Syndrome?

In my first few years as a mom, I've realized that "bad mom syndrome," or BMS, is incredibly pervasive.

I define BMS as a tendency to readily and easily call yourself a bad mom. BMS is done silently in your own head, and proclaimed aloud to others. It happens with small and big infractions, like forgetting baby wipes or having trouble breastfeeding.

You'll see BMS rear its ugly head when you or your mom friends are taking care of your own needs. If you go out with a friend who is already a mom, there is a good chance that she'll say something like "I'm such a bad mom. I left my kids at home with my husband to get a glass of wine."

As a mom-to-be, you might be raising a skeptical eyebrow, or even rolling your eyes thinking that BMS will never affect you. But BMS affects all new moms, because we hold ourselves to unrealistically high standards and the bad mom bandwagon is easy to jump on when we're sleep deprived and spent from a long day.

Trust me, there will come a time when your baby will be agitated, and you will be starving, and you'll have to choose whom to attend to first. Most of the time, you will choose to soothe your baby first, but on the occasion that you eat first and actually take care of your needs, you'll probably feel guilty and tell yourself that's not what "good moms" do.

There will also come a day when you just can't forgo a shower like you usually do because you know that having a shower will make you feel like a million bucks. And so you will leave your baby safely, but not necessarily happily in a bouncer, and you'll feel crappy for taking the time to clean your body and feel refreshed. Your brain might be telling you that you should be with your baby, entertaining and stimulating them 24/7. But I'm here to tell you that it's okay to shower.

Feeling like a "bad mom" is so prevalent today. There was even a recent movie starring Kristen Bell with the same title. The pressure to do it all - exclusively breastfeed, feed your child only organic food, sacrifice ALL of your "me" time and strictly follow fill-in-the-blank method leaves new and more experienced mothers exhausted and depleted.

This intense self-sacrificing type of mothering is an easy trap for many overachieving and career driven women to fall into, having never known how to give anything less than 200%.

As overachieving women, we are often our own worst critics, and beat ourselves up because we don't measure up against the impossible standards that we set. We want to look Instagram-perfect after a 14-hour labor, have an impeccably tidy home, be a welcoming hostess to our guests, and fit perfectly into our skinny jeans a week after birth. However, it's unrealistic to have these expectations during the most vulnerable and sleep deprived time of our lives.

Believing that we should be perfect as new mothers is easy because there are so many cultural messages around us that reinforce this. During pregnancy and as new moms, mothers get conflicting messages from society, friends and family, as well as a general onslaught of other's opinions. The information overload makes it hard to quiet the noise in our heads, and it's difficult to tap into our inner wisdom.

But have no fear, there is good news here. We've outgrown the self-sacrificing mother ideal - a mom with no needs of her own, always giving, giving, giving and ending up depleted and overwhelmed.

I'm going to fill you in on a little secret: when you become a mom, you don't stop being YOU.

Being the best mom you can be without falling into the perfection trap is a process of unlearning, and it takes time.

It's not about a Pinterest perfect birthday party, a envy inducing Instagram photo, or never getting angry - it's a whole new attitude to embrace. One that allows you to experience more joy, less judgment and more freedom. Who doesn't want that?

CHAPTER 4

Your Guide to Maternity Leave

Iwrote this 10 step guide to help new moms feel a little less overwhelmed, and a little more in control of their postnatal life.

Childbirth lasts one day (hopefully!), but motherhood is forever. This guide is here to help you prepare for the forever part.

Here are the 10 things you need to know and do as you prepare for your maternity leave.

#1 Negotiate your Leave and Request the Longest Leave Possible

First, breathe. You're not required to tell your employer that you're pregnant immediately. Use the first few months as an opportunity to gather information. Search your intranet to find out how many weeks/months you're entitled to. If there's nothing there, talk to someone in Human Resources.

If you know any women who have taken maternity leave within your company, engage them in casual conversation about how much time they took off.

Once you know what you're entitled to, and you're comfortable telling your boss that you're expecting, have a conversation about your leave with a number in mind. If you know what you're entitled to, you have stories of other women who took x number of months, and you've saved up your vacation days, your boss should have no issue agreeing with your number.

#2 HONOR YOUR LEAVE AND ALLOW YOURSELF TO BE OFFLINE COMPLETELY

This will involve transitioning all of your work to other colleagues and allowing yourself to be truly unavailable. Work will survive without you for the time being, and you will survive without work temporarily.

Assume that you are going to be completely unavailable for at least the first 6 weeks. Set that boundary up front by telling your boss and colleagues that you won't be checking your email at all for a certain amount of time.

Yes, setting expectations and boundaries is very uncomfortable. As women, we're expected to please others, so saying no isn't something that comes easily to us. But by doing this in advance, you save yourself the stress of having to deal with work while you're sleep deprived and adapting to life with a baby. Your colleagues will thank you in the long run.

#3 Prioritize Sleep

How many hours of sleep did you need before pregnancy? This number should be your daily goal. While it isn't possible to get that much sleep continuously with a newborn, you can start to catch up on your sleep with naps.

Try your best to get your sleep in segments that add up to your pre-pregnancy sleep needs. For example, if you need 9 hours of sleep to feel healthy and energized, perhaps you can sleep from 9-11pm (2 hours), 12-3am (3 hours), 4-6am (2 hours), and take an afternoon nap from 2-4pm (2 hours). Each day will be different, but aim for your sleep goal as your #1 self-care priority.

You might be wondering: How am I going to prioritize sleep with a newborn? One idea is to talk with your partner before the baby is born and ask them if they could do the last feeding of the evening so that you can go to bed early. If you have close friends or family around, ask someone to watch your baby for an hour or two, so that you can nap uninterrupted.

And if you're unable to sleep, even though you have created these times for rest, you might want to seek out a therapist[2] to support you. Not being able to rest, even when you have time to, can be a sign of postpartum depression and anxiety.[3]

And the longer you go without sleep, the more intense your symptoms can become.

As a new mom, the advice "sleep when the baby sleeps," is more difficult than it sounds. You'll likely worry about when your little one will wake up. If that's the case, try resting with your baby close by. Practicing meditation[4] can be restorative, and you can feel rejuvenated even if you don't fall asleep. (I promise you'll have to try really hard NOT to fall asleep if you listen to the Wise Mama relaxing sleep meditation! The appendix has a link for FREE streaming access.)[5]

You might find tools[6] like sleep meditation, aromatherapy, earplugs, and deep belly breathing techniques helpful to ease into sleep. Think about what you'll need to rest well (i.e., dark room, pillow, or earplugs). It might seem excessive now, but allocate areas in your home to rest during the day (i.e., sofa, guest room) and night (your room, the baby's room).

#4 TALK WITH YOUR PARTNER, EVEN ABOUT THE STUFF THAT'S HARD TO TALK ABOUT

Taking care of a baby is overwhelming for new moms, as well as for new dads. Try talking about your expectations ahead of time, as a lot of the conflict post baby will be around different opinions about what each other's expectations are. For example, as a new mom, you'll want to know if your partner is willing/able to help you with the last feeding or night shifts. Likewise, your partner will need to know if this is what you are expecting. If you have this conversation, as well as other difficult conversations before baby is born, you'll save yourself some bickering.

As a new mom, it's important to remember that your partner still needs to get their basic needs met (like sleep), and that the transition to parenthood will be challenging for them as well. Knowing how much sleep your partner needs to feel functional in a 24-hour period will be helpful.

A conversation that you need to have before the baby arrives is whether your partner will take time off from work right away, or wait until family and friends have gone home. You might prefer to spread out the care, and want your partner to take leave after your relatives depart. However, if you feel the first few weeks will be the hardest for you, you might want your partner around with your family to have "all hands on deck."

Below are some questions that you can ask your partner to get the conversation flowing about what life will be like post baby and what you both can expect from each other.

- Are you taking any type of paternity leave? If so, when will you go back to work?

- When you are back at work, who will be helping to support me when you are gone?

- Are you able to work from home at all?

- What time will you get home most evenings?

- If you are going to be more than 15 minutes later than expected, will you text me?

- Will you be waking up at night for bottle feedings or not on work nights? Or will we switch nights?

- Or if I'm breastfeeding, will you do the diaper changing and burping after I feed the baby?

Remember, you're on the same team and both adjusting to the demands of your new baby, so be patient with yourself and each other. Sometimes the partner assumes the mom always knows what to do to calm the baby. This can be a lot of pressure! It's helpful to remember that when your party is off-duty, to really let the other person rest. If mom is taking a break, but has to give step-by-step instructions the entire time, this isn't a real break. This also means that mom needs to let go (if necessary, leave the house) and let her partner learn on their own, and develop their own style of parenting.

#5 THROW AWAY YOUR MILE HIGH EXPECTATIONS

Newborns are adorable and a miracle in their own right. When your baby is born, you will find yourself being in awe of the fact that you created a life! These moments of awe will come and go, but your first weeks will be consumed by changing diapers, getting your baby to sleep, feeding your baby, and taking care of your most basic needs (shower, food, and sleep).

A good tip is to lower your expectations and to let go of what you believe life "should" be as a parent before the baby arrives. It's extremely probable that if you believe you "should" be able to go out to dinner at least once a week as a new parent that your greatest challenge as a new parent will be going to a restaurant. If you're convinced that your baby will be a good sleeper, (because why wouldn't they?), it's quite possible that your baby will wake up every hour on the hour.

The less expectations you have as a new parent, the less likely you're going to feel like a failure, bad mom, or like your baby is "difficult" when things don't go as planned. For example, there will come a time where you'll be at your wits end because your baby just...won't...stop...crying. After having changed a diaper, fed, and tried to put your baby to sleep, you will have the option to either hope that your baby stops crying, and get more and more frustrated, or just accept the fact that you've tried, that there's nothing wrong with you or the baby, and that you deserve a five or ten minute break before you attempt to calm your baby down. Again. This will get easier with practice. I promise.

Another helpful tactic is to trade expectations for appreciation of what is. Look around, and then ask yourself this powerful question: "what's not wrong right now?" and write five things down.

Shifting away from your expectations, into appreciation can help flood your body with feel good hormones. And let's be honest. Doing something other than taking care of your baby's basic needs and yours will feel like you've just run a marathon. And won.

The daily postpartum checklist (see next chapter) is also helpful for resetting your expectations. And remember that checking off a single item on the list is a WIN! It might seem ridiculous now, but "just" feeding yourself and your baby for the day can be a jam-packed and exhausting day. If you manage to squeeze in a shower, that's an amazing postnatal day.

Please give yourself the emotional and mental space for your postpartum experience to be whatever it will be— both positive and negative. Don't expect life to be anything like it was before you became a mom. And no matter what happens, you'll find your new normal in time. You may become a mom overnight, but it takes a while for the rest of your life to catch up.

#6 FIND YOUR WORKING MOM TRIBE

Write down the names of your friends that are already working parents that you see eye-to-eye with, as well as any friends that are pregnant around the same time as you. If none of your friends are parents, or pregnant, "mommy and me" groups, pre and post natal yoga, baby boot camp classes, and breastfeeding groups are a great way to meet new people. If your pre-baby life is quite hectic, social media also offers you the opportunity to connect with like-minded parents, without having to add more "stuff" to your schedule. You can join the private Wise Mama tribe on

Facebook,[7] to jump in on conversations with mamas that share your values.

A great thing to do is to reach out to three of your closest friends and talk with them about how they can best support you after your baby is born. You may even want to send them some version of the following note, or have a similar conversation over tea.

(Example: As I approach my baby's due date, I wanted to reach out and let you know that although I'm very excited to meet my baby, I'm also a little nervous about this big change. I feel like I'm going to need your support more than ever, and I'd love to know that I can reach out to you when sh*t hits the fan, or gets all over the wall as I've heard that can happen! Can you check in with me and make sure to ask me how I'm really doing and if I'm having a hard time? I know just chatting with you will make me feel better.)

#7 GET COMFORTABLE ASKING FOR HELP

You've probably heard the phrase, "It takes a village to raise a child." If you're not a parent, queue the eye roll. But parents everywhere agree with this saying. As a new mom, you don't have to do it alone, and it's very unlikely that your partner or family expect you to. So when you need help, ask for it. Don't expect your hubby, family, and friends to be mind readers and know that you're struggling.

As women, we can feel that asking for help is a weakness, or that we're not good enough. However, the opposite is true. It shows immense strength and emotional maturity to know your needs and to vocalize them. All moms who've made it through the first year or even the first few months, know how hard it is to care for a newborn. I urge you to reach out to them, even if you don't know them that well. Just hearing "it will get better," or "this is just a phase," is incredibly therapeutic. Make asking for help a habit by asking someone to help you at least once day. And yes, it's best to start this today so that you get used to the feelings that arise when you ask for help. It can be uncomfortable, especially if this is a new skill for you.

If you find yourself having an especially challenging time, it can be helpful to review the common symptoms of postpartum mood disorders on the Postpartum Support Internal Website,[8] and then meet with a therapist who specializes in maternal mental health.

Postpartum depression is more common than you think, as it affects one in seven women who give birth each year, and can occur anytime in the first year following childbirth. If you find yourself suffering like I did (see my TEDx Talk[9] for the whole story), know it's not your fault and that you will get better, but please seek professional help immediately. You don't need to suffer in silence.

#8 PLAN FOR MORE HELP THAN YOU THINK YOU NEED

Have you thought about who will do the cooking, cleaning, and laundry once you get home from the hospital? Perhaps you can get your friends and family to cook you weekly meals so that you have leftovers, and have only to reheat your food. Instead of a baby shower, maybe you can gather your friends for a cook-a-thon, and stuff your freezer with healthy meals that you and partner can have post-baby. Additionally, maybe your parents or in laws can help you do laundry? If you don't have a cleaner, maybe it's time to get one on a weekly rotation. If you don't have any family nearby or even if you do, think about hiring a postpartum doula for those first few weeks after birth.

It's vital that you rest and recover from childbirth. Although this process is natural, your body has just created a life, and delivered it (i.e., taken a beating). You wouldn't run 10 miles the day after completing a marathon, so don't overdo it after childbirth. Many women outside of the US are supported post-delivery by their families and communities, and are not allowed to do any housework and chores for the first month. Your family and friends will want to help, but you'll need to let them know what you need. To help make being supported by others feel more natural, check out this receiving support meditation.[10] And remember how good it feels to help others. You are not being needy; you are giving others a chance to feel great.

Whether it's a postpartum doula, night nurse, babysitter, mother's helper, lactation consultant, house cleaner or chef, find people in your area and make a budget for what you can afford and whom you'd like to hire. Remember, the first few months are the hardest, and this period doesn't last forever. So if you need help, get it. The investment in your sanity is worth it. You can checkout out DONA International[11] to find a list of postpartum doulas in your area. Also, TaskRabbit is helpful for eclectic needs, and UrbanSitter and Care.com are helpful spots to look for babysitters.

#9 Practice Mindfulness

Mindfulness is such a buzzword these days, it can create all sorts of complicated ideas in our minds. The concept of mindfulness is quite simple in theory, but can be difficult in practice.

Mindfulness is the state of awareness that arises from intentionally paying attention to the present moment, without judgment. Basically it's a state of mind that arises when you're actually focused on doing what you're doing, and not wishing it were different.

Sounds simple, yet, when holding a crying baby, practicing mindfulness can seem out of reach since all we want to do is calm the baby down. We probably have many thoughts *(I just changed the baby's diaper and fed her. Why is the she crying again? I bet Leslie's baby doesn't wail like this, I must be doing something wrong)* pulling us away from the direct experience of the sounds the baby is making, the weight of the baby in our arms, the gentle rise and fall of the baby's chest. When we can practice mindfulness, we hear the baby's crying, but also remain centered and know that this is the way our baby is trying to communicate with us.

One way to increase mindfulness is to practice meditation, so that you start to train your brain to pay attention to the present moment. One of the most simple meditations you can practice is to pay attention to your breath. Every time you catch your mind wandering away from the breath (it will!), and you bring your attention back, it's like a bicep curl for your brain. Repeat these "reps" for a few minutes until you're ready to end your practice. Studies have shown that as little as five minutes a day can start to have measurable impact, so don't be afraid to start small. Mindfulness Based Achievement, the company I co-founded, has a free 30 Day Meditation Challenge that you can check out on our website;[12] you'll receive a daily email with a short 5 minute guided meditation.

Mindfulness also helps to remind us that "this too shall pass," and "this is only temporary" and these are saving graces for all new moms out there.

#10 PRACTICE SELF-COMPASSION

I must admit that I was extremely skeptical of the power of Self-Compassion and even went as far as to think that it was problematic and self-indulgent. I figured if I was too nice to myself, then I'd let myself off the hook and would never strive to do anything great again. I thought I would become lazy and just settle for "ok."

The opposite is true.

According to Kristin Neff,[13] a researcher on the topic, Self-Compassion is comprised of three elements: self-kindness, common humanity, and mindfulness.

Fostering self-kindness helps us stop judging ourselves too harshly, common humanity helps us realize that life can be tough sometimes, and mindfulness reduces our tendency to exaggerate or ruminate on problems.

In essence, Self-Compassion is the opposite of letting ourselves off the hook, it's simply looking at our struggles at face value, and then talking to ourselves the way a friend would.

Take a five minute Self-Compassion break now[14] and see how it makes you feel. This guided audio recording will walk you through all three steps of practicing Self-Compassion in a short five minute meditation.

Want to go even further and get additional support as your transition into motherhood? Head to WiseMama.co[15] to join the Wise Mama Tribe and get FREE access to the first lesson of Rock Your Maternity Leave & Bounce Back,[16] the official Wise Mama course.

CHAPTER 5

Your New To-Do List While on Maternity Leave

One of the hardest things about transitioning into motherhood is that you're probably used to knocking out your to-do list and getting stuff done. Achievement, efficiency and order have always been your strong suits. It's hard to imagine that things will change when you're on maternity leave, and that sending a single email can be akin to climbing Mt. Everest.

So for all of you who love your to-do lists and can't help but check things off, remember that doing just one of the these things a day is a MAJOR win.

- ☐ I asked someone for help
- ☐ I fed my baby
- ☐ I got out of bed
- ☐ I took a shower
- ☐ I ate a meal
- ☐ I read a book to my baby

- ☐ I went to my doctor's appointment today
- ☐ I took my baby to the doctor
- ☐ I sang to my baby today
- ☐ I did something just for me
- ☐ I did some self-care
- ☐ I snuggled with my baby
- ☐ I fed my baby without getting distracted by my phone or the TV
- ☐ I kissed my baby
- ☐ I let someone help me
- ☐ I shared how I'm really feeling
- ☐ I shared how I'm feeling and what I need to make things better
- ☐ I set a boundary and kept it
- ☐ I said "no" to something
- ☐ I shared my preferences and said no to something that I didn't like
- ☐ I accepted imperfection and "good enough" today
- ☐ I did something that was hard for me
- ☐ I acknowledged that I'm not ok, and that's ok
- ☐ I left the house today
- ☐ I went for a walk
- ☐ I got dressed today

☐ I called a friend today

☐ I stopped doing something that was not supporting me (Googling random things/mindless Facebook scrolling/etc.)

☐ I meditated today

☐ I noticed my chest rising and falling and then my baby's chest doing the same thing

☐ I took one long deep breath

☐ I took a break

☐ I took five minutes for me

☐ I took my vitamins today

☐ I laughed today

☐ I spoke up for myself today

☐ I spoke kindly to myself today

☐ My baby was cared for today (even if it wasn't by me)

☐ I was patient with myself today

☐ I bathed my baby today

☐ I didn't get poop on myself

☐ I confided in a friend

☐ I was honest with my partner

☐ I let myself release my emotions and have a good cry

You have so much to look forward to with the birth of your little one. Being a mom might very well be the most meaningful and gratifying experience of your life, but it might not be exactly what you expected, especially in the early days. But no matter what, remember to rely on your family and community, your inner wisdom, as well as the steps I've laid out here to best prepare you for the exciting journey you're about to embark on.

And let's keep the conversation going, head to WiseMama.co[17] to join the Wise Mama Tribe and get FREE access to the first lesson of Rock Your Maternity Leave & Bounce Back,[18] the official Wise Mama course. I'd be honored to continue supporting you along your journey.

Appendix

For access to the following links,
please visit: www.wisemama.co/appendix

1. Burnout: The High Cost of High Achievement by Freudenberger: www.bit.ly/burnoutbook

2. Therapists and Maternal Mental Health Specialists: www.bit.ly/maternahealth

3. Signs of Postpartum Depression and Anxiety: www.bit.ly/postpartumPPD

4. Mindfulness Based Achievement Free 30 Day Meditation Challenge: www.bit.ly/MBA30day

5. Wise Mama Relaxing Sleep Meditation: www.wisemama.co/book-sleep-meditation

6. Wise Mama Sleep Accessories and Tools: www.wisemama.co/sleep-accessories

7. Join the Private Wise Mama Tribe on Facebook: www.bit.ly/wisemamaFB

8. Common Symptoms of Postpartum Mood Disorders: www.bit.ly/postpartumPPD

9. Lisa Abramson's TEDx Talk: www.bit.ly/TEDxLisa

10. Wise Mama Receiving Support Meditation: www.wisemama.co/receiving-support

11. Find a List of Postpartum Doulas through DONA International: www.bit.ly/doulafinder

12. Mindfulness Based Achievement Free 30 Day Meditation Challenge: www.bit.ly/MBA30day

13. Self-Compassion: The Proven Power of Being Kind to Yourself by Neff: www.bit.ly/NeffCompassion

14. Wise Mama Five Minute Self-Compassion Break Meditation: www.wisemama.co/self-compassion-meditation

15. Wise Mama Website: www.wisemama.co

16. FREE Access to The First Lesson of Rock Your Maternity Leave & Bounce Back, the Official Wise Mama Course: www.wisemama.co/free-class

17. Wise Mama Website: www.wisemama.co

18. Free Access to The First Lesson of Rock Your Maternity Leave & Bounce Back, the Official Wise Mama Course: www.wisemama.co/free-class

19. Lisa Abramson's Executive Coaching and Speaking Website: www.lisaabramson.com

20. Wise Mama Website: www.wisemama.co

21. Mindfulness Based Achievement Website: www.mindfulnessbasedachievement.com

22. List of 100 Most Influential Leaders Empowering Women Worldwide by EBW22: www.ebw2020.com/ebw-100

23. Fast Company: 5 Ways To Lean In Without Burning Out: www.bit.ly/FastCoLeanIn

24. Lisa Abramson's TEDx Talk: www.bit.ly/TEDxLisa

Disclaimer: The information and resources available in this book are not a substitute for medical evaluation, treatment, or consultation. Any answers to questions posed and any recommendations or information provided therein should not be used as a substitute for medical or relevant other advice by physicians and/or mental health professionals. Wise Mama has an affiliate revenue relationship with Amazon. If you see a link to a retailer, please assume that it is an affiliate link. However, rest assured that our affiliate relationships do not guide our product recommendations, at all.

Acknowledgements

A special thank you to Carolina Baker, for working her editing magic and making this book the gem it is today.

And a heartfelt thank you to Claire Mulkey for the gorgeous photography featured on the cover, and Dan Abramson for perfecting the cover design.

About The Author

Lisa Abramson[19] is an entrepreneur, executive coach and maternal mental health advocate. She founded Wise Mama[20] and co-founded Mindfulness Based Achievement,[21] the New MBA, which teaches high potential women leaders how to create sustainable success. Her MBA curriculum has been taught to hundreds of women, as well as at Google, Cisco, The Stanford Graduate School of Business, LinkedIn, YouTube, Salesforce, Microsoft and many others.

Lisa was recently honored as one of the 100 Most Influential Leaders Empowering Women Worldwide by EBW,[22] and has been featured in Fast Company, sharing 5 Ways To Lean

In Without Burning Out[23] as well as The Guardian UK, Refinery29, Lucie's List, 32/7, LifeHack, and The Mighty. She has also been a featured guest on popular podcasts like The Fourth Trimester, The MomVent, Motherbirth, Mom & Mind and The Postpartum Podcast.

An in-demand speaker, Lisa has been on stage at numerous high profile conferences including Salesforce's Dreamforce, TEDx, The Watermark Conference for Women and others. She speaks regularly at, and conducts workshops for, companies ranging from global Fortune 500s to tech start-ups. Her TEDx talk[24] on her experience with postpartum depression and psychosis has been viewed over 24,000 times.

Lisa graduated from Vanderbilt University in Nashville, TN and lives in Menlo Park, California with her husband and daughter. Connect with Lisa at lisaabramson.com

81940276R00029

Made in the USA
San Bernardino, CA
12 July 2018